New North Carolina Poetry

The Eighties

New
North Carolina Poetry

The Eighties

Selected and edited by
Stephen E. Smith

Green River Press
1982

Copyright 1983 by Stephen E. Smith

ISBN 0-940580-23-3

Printed in the United States of America

Green River Press
Saginaw Valley State College
University Center, MI 48710

To my parents --

Emerson Perry Smith
Louise McKnett Smith

Contents

Betty Adcock. Elizabeth Playing	15
Dreamed Chant	17
A. R. Ammons. Zero and Then Some	18
James Applewhite. Passing the Marquee in Maysville	20
Southland Drive-In	21
Trying to Drive Away from the Past	22
Margaret Boothe Baddour. These Geese	23
Ronald H. Bayes. Weymouth: Tokyo	24
Mary Belle Campbell. March Beach	25
Fred Chappell. Season of Transfigurement	26
The Moon Regards the Frozen Earth	27
Elizabeth Cox. Under the Hickory Nut Three	28
The Lady Cellist	30
Alan Davis. The End of the Affair	31
Barbara Rosson Davis. Shooting Stars	33
Ann Deagon. The Lesson	34
Ann Dunn. [Untitled]	35
Mildred Dunn. Carolina Gospel Old-Time Revival	36
Monday Night: Preacher	37
Charles Edward Eaton. Figures in a Compleat Season	38
Grace Gibson. Myth: To the Fourth Generation	39
Marie Gilbert. Come Fetch Me	40
Evalyn P. Gill. Allegheny Commuter Flight	41
Lucinda Grey. The Motion of What Has Happened	42
Robert Grey. Holloween	43
Kathryn Bright Gurkin. Nonagenarian	45
Tom Hawkins. Memo: How to Become a Famous Wild Man	46
Ninety-Two at Noon	47
Lois Holt. Breakin' In	48
Will Inman. Recognitions	49
David Owen Johnson. Dude Bridges	50
What	52

Paul Jones. Toward Sleep	54
Mary Kratt. On the Steep Side	55
Julian Oliver Long. Salvationists Escaping	56
Agnes McDonald. Cast/ For Jason	57
Equinox	58
Michael McFee. Homing	59
Reclamation	60
Heather Ross Miller. A Girl with Many Moving Parts	61
Leda Talks back to Zeus	63
Jim Wayne Miller. Girls Grow on Trees in Haywood County	65
Fever	67
Shirley Moody. The Painter Considers Black and White	68
Ruth Moose. Going Presbyterian	69
Robert Morgan. Fire Words	70
Stripes	71
Pamolu Oldham. Mongoloid Boy Poem, April 1981	72
Sam Ragan. For Remembering	73
Salvatore Salerno. Sappho	74
Sharon Shaw. [Untitled]	75
J. R. Simmons. Back to Scuppernongs	76
Jane K. Smith. Juke Box	77
R. T. Smith. Snapper	78
Working up a Thirst in the Hollow Log Lounge	79
Stephen E. Smith. Advice	81
Mary C. Snotherly. The Southern Fried Chicken	83
Shelby Stephenson. Look Away	84
The Rock Hole in Late April	85
Julie Suk. Don't Tell Me	86
Chuck Sullivan. The Advent of the Kingdom in Carolina	87
Kate Kelly Thomas. Maggie Yells Leroy out of Sight	88
Charles Tisdale. Winter's Last Snowstorm	89
Anna Wooten. Divorce	90
What Augustine Did with Sunlight	92
Notes	93

Foreword

As best as I can make it out, this is the story.

Once there was a land of rivershine and twigfire. It was a magical land where every Sunday's ritual/ was the same chicken, a land of plenty that hung on vines to be picked. The southern poet lived there, already as a child viewing it with a slant world eye. In the Bible Belt right here/ where nothing is/ Or could be finer, the child had an immediate askew angle of vision, knowing the secret life beneath the picnic table. He observed the life of his fathers and forefathers -- *they so old it's like they was laughing* -- and saw this life as the endless doing up of buttons, a life constrained to schedule and ritual, in a corset/ like a fine, Southern lady. There was continuity in space -- a stretch of earth, a part of the main -- as well as in time, the water of a deed/ washing other deeds.

But Time drops like a shroud. That former world is no longer with us. A different world has come, though the new lands imagined are haunted from the past, and the poet at all times feels enormously the undertow of origin. But the poet remembers; he turns away to mark it down/ For remembering, and for him That morning is still as fresh/ as the smell of green lumber.

Yet memory is not enough to anneal the fracture between Then and Now. Fence posts measure off/ the driving past; his father's world has turned and turned on him. Now this sky gives the painter difficulty, and it seems sentimental to proclaim, "The heart is everywhere." Something has broken *(Why'd you want to go and do that for?)*, and the poet must try to figure/ who done wrong and what. In present time the poet's task is the long shouldering/ of rage; he must join the asking in unison/ to please God be included. But he is not included; like silent Pound, tormented Poe, he is an outcast, one of the fallen/ angels, streaks of light, a rush/ in Southern humid night. He feels divorced from the society around, but not from history, which is as powerful as nature, powerful as the moon which pushes/ a man across a field. History is the force that will not leave off, will tell itself even upon those yet/ to be born, their faces looking back like ours.

I have tortured lines out of context in order to outline this story, but I do not think I have got the outline wrong. It is not a new story, after all, but the familiar Romantic one we heard at the knee of Wordsworth. Or maybe we heard it from Baudelaire or Henry

Vaughan. Or perhaps we read it in Genesis, where the gates of Eden closed to with a heartsickening thud. Some of my old friends -- Allen Tate, say, or Andrew Lytle -- might have suggested that this Eden was cognate not only with childhood, but also with the antebellum south. But that possibility now seems remote as childhood, remoter than Eden, and in many ways not very attractive.

I think it was the novelist Graham Greene who said, "Childhood is the writer's capital." A southern writer would probably redefine it as landed property, about which he is more fiercely protective than he is about money. As southern writers we are children *with*, as well as *of*, Huckleberry Finn, and we most treasure exactly what he treasured: a vision of personal freedom rebellious toward historical necessity. The simultaneous recognition of the victory of historical necessity over rebellion produces a vision allied to tragic vision, though the characteristic utterance of this vision is in pathos.

This historical mythos was treated directly by our immediate forbears, the Fugitive poets, who spoke of it in intellectual terms, borrowing terminology and tenor of thought from T.S. Eliot's larger and more hieratic view of history. A contemporary southern poet will immediately shuck the intellectual abstractions off this story; his poem will likely be personal, autobiographical; he will attest to no more than he has seen or experienced, and when he has an intellectual conclusion he will offer it with offhand diffidence or make a subdued ironic joke of it. His, more than any other American poetry, is likely to be humorous, genial, anecdotal.

But in large part the personal experience he reports fits pretty neatly into the Fugitive framework of history. It is as if the contemporary southern poet is backing and filling, performing laboratory experiments that shore up, illustrate, the old thesis without significantly altering it. Is this because of the poet's modern distrust of intellection? Or because the old idea is true and requires no change? Or is it a matter of ancestor worship?

No idea, not even in science, can remain valid without reinterpretation over a long period of time, and at this moment southern poetry, southern literature in general, holds its breath in anticipation. Either a new framework or a radical revision of the older is in order, and seems to be just offstage, waiting for its entrance cue. What this new aesthetic-historic picture will be is difficult to say, but one can predict with some confidence that there will be a discarding of the extremely personal note that James Dickey so flamboyantly inserted into southern poetry. There will be a broader inclusion of urban landscape and sensibility; perhaps a poetry *of* the Lost World, rather than *about* it, is to be born. Southern poetry, which has always been less provincial, more international, than other American regional poetries may now begin to turn its back on French, Spanish, and Latin American poetry, though with gratitude and regret. Maybe even the customary splendid rhetoric is in line to have its neck wrung.

All that is speculation, as gossamer as reflected moonlight.

What is certain is that if new views, new structures, do show up, there shall be poets equipped to articulate them. This selection of "New North Carolina Poetry" was made from some 800-odd submissions. The poets here represented have, then, some reason to congratulate themselves, but I do not see that those excluded have much reason to be downcast. The level of quality among North Carolina poets is extraordinary, and I am at a loss to account for it.

The remark currently making the rounds -- that Carolina poets write good poems and New York poets write good grant proposals -- may be flatly true, for all I know. In this selection we see poems various and vigorous, in a ferment of change, not passively waiting. And -- wonder of wonders -- here is a poetry confident of its powers, goodnatured in its outlook. It is a poetry with a future, as well as an evident past.

-- Fred Chappell

Betty Adcock

ELIZABETH, PLAYING

Colored sticks leap from her hand, settle
among marbles cloudy with rose and yellow.
All of an hour she has tossed and made these
be other, out of her hands.
Bumps on the bedspread have marked her thighs.
She rubs how the skin knows
where it's been.
The grandfather comes through the screendoor streaming
late sun off his shoulders,
thunking his cane in the corner. "It's coming
a rain. Heard the east thunder."
She knows there can be no weather
until he tells it.

So the red stick she holds is already
old, even its nearness to becoming
something else for her sake already lost
in what rain is: the wet chickens coming
in their smell of ashes, the brick walk
washed dark and slick, the cistern pinging.
She is stopped barely hearing
the radio hum its *somewhere
in the Pacific.*

No one she knows is in the places
the radio talks. She is here.
Far back in the house, the grandmother
clinks in the kitchen, under its one-eye.
Lightbulb on a string sways there.
It can throw her shadow farther than the rope swing goes.
She thinks that shadow
out the back door all the way to the cows.

Yard-weeds lean away from the wet
that is coming. In the screendoor, the sun
shuts its eye, nightbugs
burring where the light was.

She wants —
is it to taste this?
Wet brick, pink bedspread, feather, firepoker,
rocker varnished with salt,
her tongue knows how each tastes like itself.
Herself, a mouth on her knuckle.

What is so important that it shuts her throat?

Not even the big marble hurting her knee
can make her move. She is spread
over everything like its own taste,
the way rain will be over everything,
is, and everything is together the way her toes
are on her feet, her arms on her shoulders,
an ache in all of it, this keeping.

Should she cry? The grandfather's listening
to the Pacific, his pipe sparkling.
This, this, she whispers and waits.
It is only summer and dusk. But might
something fumble and miss? Might the furniture
run away like the dog or the roof crumple down,
the hens come apart, or the grandfather, grandfather —
like the handful of sticks?
*If I have to call something back
what will it be, can I choose, and what name?*

She is still as she knows to be, the toys
rocking a little with her breath;
and the hard thunder turns over black;
the quick marbles fall, rolling under the bed.
She remembers the name;
dead is the name she remembers, wakes
to the drum of the rain
as it breaks its long sticks
in the dark, on the round world rolling.

Betty Adcock

DREAMED CHANT

Three quarters
Lidded moon in liveoak's ladder
Wakes to the call of the owl-daughter.

She is she who called our fathers
Where they waited out the red-feathered
Fox by rivershine and twigfire,
Fox that narrowed and answered never
The long question of the hunter
Though moon spread like blood on water
And the wild crucifix of geese passed over.

Escaped alone, the fox in his bright hair
Turns, hangs a new moon in the tree's fingers,
Hides a name in the owl's quaver
Twists brushfire through the year's weather.

Whose hound's cry rides our dark like a mane of fever?

A. R. Ammons

ZERO AND THEN SOME

We would not want to persuade ourselves
on eternity with an insistence of
our own, pre-empting narrowly or

warping out of centrality the nature of what is —
nevertheless we would not want to miss a
right praising, even if we had to reduce

the praise from substance and stand empty
in stance alone, an attitude merely or
willingness that would at least shirk

indifference in wanting not to avoid praise:
whatever forever is we would not want to be
unconjoined with it or only in the ways

the temporal and particular necessarily
fall short of staying put: there is
an ongoing we nearly cheapen by being its

specific crest, but humbly we know too it
bore us and will support us into whatever
rest remains: what if the infinite

filters through here ordinary as if it
were just taking place locally? that is,
though the infinite is quite impressive

it may be like a weak gravity field, the
least spectacular thing around, the
immediate's most trifling ingredient: we

probably couldn't detect it to redress or
address it, amass it to praise it, not with
regular human instrumentation: but addle

us enough, we will drop the whole
subject and invent for substitution "that
which is to be praised"   and invest it with

our store of verve, not matter: the jay
will sometimes at dawn sit in the blue spruce
as if too blank to stir first and

piddle idly in song like a swinging
squeak or singing wheel: it could be praise
though how it works or why it's sung, we guess.

James Applewhite

PASSING THE MARQUEE IN MAYSVILLE

Storefronts cardboard in streetlight
And shadow, moviehouse midway the stoplights.
Shirley Temple wore her lily dresses
On screen. Linda Blair, Brooke Shields,
Kristy McNichol, publicly unbosom
In whorehouse scripts, consigned to the devil.
What quality of face in the stripling,
Like Huckleberry Finn with tits,
Crossing into night where the red light held,
Exploitable water of innocence
Already dry behind those eyes?
What do we extract from their precocious screams —
Some slick bright thing like sap from a stem?
I remember as a child in an overgrown
Yard, absently striking the lilies
In a luxury of violation.

James Applewhite

SOUTHLAND DRIVE-IN

This is the obligatory Southern poem.
Will copperheads horny with venom twine
Cornerstones of mansions left charred by Sherman?
Listen, the field is paved, the only crop
Raised these speakers on poles. They crackle
With rumor, to boys with hand on the stick-shift,
Of the virgin who died impaled, after
Coca-Cola laced with Spanish Fly.
Fried chicken is eaten, not all the meat
Here is white, but even as a thunderhead
Slashes and cannonades, rendering heat
Into current, this living theater of bodies
Plays out its music, like a radio tuned
To a station from so far away, maybe
Latin America, its reception sounds eerie
With static and distance. Antennas catch
Signals from ditches, where frogs no bigger
Than the gonad-shaped pecans of the grove
Blow their bellies up to broadcast:
They say from the water, *we all here is*
Dark meat. Blacks run away to the swamps,
Slick with the rapes you wish your sisters.
The root of this plot, upraised on the screen
Is poor white meat. And a wind comes
Sighing from the crowd, the great thundercrowd
In the mind of this Southern land. Some rain
Has fallen, little rivers trickled on the banks
Of back seats. Moccasins slide a soft water.

James Applewhite

TRYING TO DRIVE AWAY FROM THE PAST

Wastes of my life reflect from these clay flats
    With fennel as from plate glass windows:
Barber shops — emporia for pimples, white wall
    Haircuts, jokes about new uses for the tongue.
Today, where branches seem wrought Spanish railings,
    The cliff-face woodland opens in. I see
Countries more essential than any I've suspected,
    With well-ordered forest slopes and deer.
Such fantasies follow from the pewter, copper green,
    The antique leather, of a few last leaves —
Though the new lands imagined are haunted by the past.
    Though the fields here are peopled with faces,
Misery and poverty I can never do anything about.
    Basketball goals in projects hand rim-bent,
With white threads of nets, like a thousand-time
    Shredded virginity, the boys who played so often
Still one-on-one, eyeball to eyeball.
    Their score is still nothing to nothing.

Margaret Boothe Baddour

THESE GEESE

Having dreamed them all year
we hesitate to see them, full feather,
perched on the bridge, dotting the pond.
But they never change, these geese,
only the swan has found a partner
and some miscegenation of Canada geese
with ducks produced a gaggle of misfits —
too long-necked to be one, too white
to be another. From this safe green place
we ponder silent Pound, tormented Poe
and all the small lost poets.
Plunging their necks below, the swans
lift triangle tails to fish for food.

Ronald H. Bayes

WEYMOUTH: TOKYO

This particular bird
says "ki-ku — ki-ku"
all the time.

Teru
I remember too
ki-ku — ki-ku.

Sloppy as it
reads "The heart
is everywhere."

Mary Belle Campbell

MARCH BEACH

Last night
the earth on line
between the pull
of sun
and full moon
brought on
a nor'easter
with the peak
tide.

Rain and waves
pounded
battered
beach walls
ripped the dunes.

This morning
I climb the ridge to
blue sky.

The steps to the beach
the sea oats
gone.
The neighbors' dunes
clawed out to sea.

Homes perch like gulls.
Pelicans glide
above a white shore.
A stretch of the earth
a part of the main
gnawed away
this morning's sea
calm.

Fred Chappell

SEASON OF TRANSFIGUREMENT

Welter and wither are wealthy on the mountain.
The colors of horses infest the whiteoaks,
The corn comes home to die.
                            Take your sweet time,
Muskrat, the creek is creeping easy,
Moonshadow purples the water.

All across the sky the hoohaw aurora,
The new Ice Age, the barn swallows crossing.
Ice Age a narrow sleep like old pineboard,
That sleep alert as the mousing owl
And silent as the hushabye cloud.

The land stretches out in stupor like a stone ogre.
The idle of stars over cut-glass tombstones.

For the first time in my death,
I feel myself a lone figure.

Fred Chappell

THE MOON REGARDS THE FROZEN EARTH

Are you, my sister, done at last
With your green and foolish frippery,
Deciding that bone white is best
To wed the proud Eternity?

So I decided long ago,
And I must say, *I told you so.*

Elizabeth Cox

UNDER THE HICKORY NUT THREE

for Ozella

The black face ate the persimmons whole,
a juice running slack and thin down her mouth.
The white child tasted the hickory
fallen from our oldest tree,
and stories dropped all day
from the black woman's soft, blunt face.
Her fingers could pull back the husks
to feed the child who wished to touch

her palms that smelled like wood,
or the half-moons of her fingernails.
Neither knew how to talk
of what was mounting under the tongue:
a hickory worked inside their words,
through years of days and nights
when the child would walk in sleep
to the room, the lamp that burned all night,

and slip beneath the covers
where a drowsy black pulse
carried them toward morning.
And they spoke of what they wished for,
what could be found at the hickory nut tree
or in the taste of persimmons
that lay cold beneath the tongue,
like a coin lodged there forever.

Now you listen to me,
when they cut down that tree,
you gonna count those rings,
you gonna see how they go out so far,
telling you how old they is,
and they so old it's like they was laughing,
like they was somebody down in there
that can't stop laughing.

When the crickets came at noon,
they rubbed their scream like saws
against a different wood.
Ozella knew how trees were cut.
She taught me to eat persimmons whole,
to wear for Sunday around my neck
the clover chains we wove all day.
When she took me home, she bathed me good.

Those stumps lay flat and round today,
and rings of certain age start there,
where somebody deep inside the wood
throws back her head
as if she could never stop the laughing.
And the crickets have already come,
but they have not broken the chain we wove,
they have not taken the coin lodged under the tongue.

Elizabeth Cox

THE LADY CELLIST

Your hair is long as the cello,
Your legs prop open, your neck
Beside its neck, holds like a lover.
A history imagined, but dim.
One wrist breaks the air, elbow out,
Your whole head bowed.
A washerwoman bending over her tub,
She scrubs her children's clothes.

Beside her, a willow spreads
Like a small bush. A boy learns
To ride his bike on the road. He reaches
The stand of pine without falling.
That night at the concert hall,
You knew what you were doing,
Each round borne deep inside those strings,
Your fingers must have burned.

A field of folk applauds the chords
That rose inside the board you scrubbed.
Fat ridges rubbed the collar clean. Your dress
Falls between your knees like a sail, loosened
From wind, light and shade shifting
Like wrens. Your fingers seek no name,
No road. Bend over your tub of clothes.
And fields rest in sounds they love.

Alan Davis

THE END OF THE AFFAIR

What doesn't kill us
makes us strong
she said
on the rosary beads
of her fingers, fluttering
silhouettes tapping
latticed shelves —
the open refrigerator's
bare bulb
hummed
its low-rent mantra.
Her voice threaded
its litany, knitted
her free
from the glare —
his frown, baked
into enamel, wiped clean
from baseboard
with the persistence
of moths
drawn to the glow
of any gleaming twitter
of light or wool —
any secret line
to tie around her heartload
of luggage, string
to bare walls.
Whiffs of freon
curl
to where a blue oasis
of curtain once billowed.

Vast deserts of hardwood floor
and this mirage —
all that's left
of what they fled from
years after vowing
it would last forever.
They stepped
out, parched and thirsting
for a change
from the frayed coat
still hanging in the closet
the bathroom slippers
quickly silvered by sun and dust
near the porcelain tub.

Barbara Rosson Davis

SHOOTING STARS

Tonight the frozen remnants from
the crumbling comet Swift Tuttle
from fifty shooting stars
an hour across the dark,
igniting night and eye.
The constellation Perseus sparks
these zooming meteors — fallen
angels, streaks of light, a rush
in Southern humid night.

Ann Deagon

THE LESSON

      for Julian

The cat teaches what she knows:
how the bones come out of hiding,
how the sun where she lies
couchant, the couch her bier,
melts all but skull away.
Food offerings untouched.
Fed water drop by drop.
(The daughter of the house,
her age-mate, both nineteen,
tends her and mourns.)
                      The light
across her like a net
from diamond window-panes
and pendent chandelier
lead crystal behind glass
a sheen of sterling, all
focus on her. Sanctum.
Umbilicus. Black Hole.
She narrows to a slit
through which it pours, our world.
The crystal does not break:
it elongates and flows.
The cat is teaching
what she knows.

Ann Dunn

(UNTITLED)

The third baby, who died,
Came with the Iris.
Every wild thing is possible in formal gardens.
I planted her behind the boxwood hedge
And in the months of bulb-splitting
Filled my mouth with dirt.

At night I pulled her from between my legs
And gave her winning names:
Ice Sculpture, Loudon Beauty, Royal Ballet,
Miss Indiana, Blue Lustre, Vanity,
Night Raider, Lillibulero, Lady Already,
And Flamenco.

What a life she would have led.
I still hold my fist
Away up between my legs
Pretending the drought
Didn't get her,
And unfold purple fingers every Spring.

Millard Dunn

CAROLINA GOSPEL OLD-TIME REVIVAL

                Sunday Night: Youth Group

The heat in the church waits
as still as I thought prayer should
be: I count the hymns left to
sing: when the music
starts, a breeze sneaks through
the open double doors at the back
of the church, and washes me
clean in the blood of
July. Outside, tree frogs sing
their own hymns, ignorant
of the hallelujah and amen we sing,
ignorant, too, of the chilling sweat
that beads in the wet bight
between the shoulder blades of Jeanette Morgan,
chin up, chest out, singing
half a light year away, two pews
in front of me.

Millard Dunn

MONDAY NIGHT: PREACHER

For a month these services have hung
from every telephone pole between Raeford
and Pinehurst, with my name in huge letters
and my picture looking as if God

stood inside my skull, counting
the house. Lord, I am not
certain, and my father's world
has turned and turned on me.

When I was a child, we sang
on the lawn for a blessing, drank
bitter iced tea, ate country ham
and chocolate pie before we went

inside, to listen to my father.
Who tried to tell us that, if
we turned loose of ourselves, we'd
fall into a deep well, a well

that each self was only the rim
of, and at the bottom we'd find
ourselves as new as when we
step, steaming and soapy, from a tub

of scalding water. I knew
he would not lie to me, and turned
loose, and am still falling.
Perhaps I could not, even then,

let go the rim, and all my life
have only dreamed of falling.

Charles Edward Eaton

FIGURES IN A COMPLEAT SEASON

The summer is replete when I conceive
The tall, dark woman with the bouffant hair
Sitting among huge watermelon slices
As though she intended a lush still life,
Small, controlled, but it got away from her,
Enlarging on its own a bright image-world —
There is a swamped sense of inundation
As if she must ride a curved, meat-filled ship
Or flood out on an ocean of pink juice.
This is what happens to these dark women
Who cut into a melon on the table,
Counting on little lipstick smears of color,
A blue dish if the patient really bleeds:
They are sorcerers of the arranged life,
Salome's sisters with their neat, quartered heads —
I used to see them on summer porches,
Their powerful hands passing out communion
To men with the unexposed white bellies,
The underside of fruit sun could not reach,
Hitching their suspenders and spitting seeds,
Sending out some black telegraphic code.
But the women never heard the S.O.S.,
And only the child saw how the summer
Turned on them, threatened loose ships, a wild pink sea —
Now I can never smell a warm melon
In the sun without this protuberant sense
Of secret life beneath the picnic table —
I cling to the dark legs of sorcerers
I plead with the pale side to turn over,
A swollen image wanting so much more.

Grace Gibson

MYTH: TO THE FOURTH GENERATION

> "We face the past; it may be shadowy,
> but it is all there is." — Northrop Frye

No one lives in the house on that rocky
hill since the last child died, but I sometimes
go back with my sons and in dreams, real to
me as myth. Old photos glimpsed in albums
children open like Swiss music boxes
for their tinkling tunes implode in sudden
recognition. See that aquiline nose
how that eyebrow flares, dark curly hair that
comb and water cannot slick down; boys in
brass-buttoned uniforms posed on the front
stoop with laughing girls in long white dresses.
We are theirs. They gaze at us like mirrors.

The snapshot group breaks up, turns away from
the box Kodak. They grow older, change, turn
into trees, become fixed stars, sow dragon's
teeth, cast thunderbolts, make the weather of
this place. For my boys the hollow house, like
some serene museum, preserves the empty
stage of an ended world. I can still hear
the cannon, caught in the crossfire, see old
battles won or lost, hear the silence hum.
To defuse our day, we look for those yet
to be born, their faces looking back like ours.

Marie Gilbert

COME FETCH ME

The tall shadow is gone
from this playing ground
leaving keen cut
silhouette sharper than life.

A sweater draping the swing strap
I am left
all through the night drizzle
dripping red from my weave.
With morning, the fabric will dry,
stiffen in the sun.

Evalyn P. Gill

ALLEGHENY COMMUTER FLIGHT

All life should hover over Philadelphia,
a watchful cormorant above the prize
destined for capture —
sunlight gems of color parked to please the eye,
white storage discs like tantalizing mints,
fast angel fish of foam along the Delaware
fantailing tugs to sea.
Kaleidescopic patches on the ground
lure predatory eye and mind.

And then the paradox of progress,
brush of island green
looms bright within the river's ribboned brown.

Lucinda Grey

THE MOTION OF WHAT HAS HAPPENED

A car skids in beside the ambulance.
The passenger door flung open,
a woman's trembling leg braces against the ground
trying to stop the motion
of what has happened —
her son's wife mutilated on the floor,
the son with blood on his hands.

I think of
Tess lying on the slab at Stonehenge,
Anna fallen under the train,
and Hester Prynne,
all loved by men unable to love them.

And when I think of you,
my tongue returns again
to the space where the tooth was taken out
that shouldn't hurt anymore,
but does.

Robert Grey

HOLLOWEEN

Sprawled by a hissing fire
we stab, gouge, scrape, empty,
sketch and slice — alert
for cavities and soft spots.
Each pumpkin has one chance
to have its ingrown features
read correctly. Having done
our best, we set them in position —
committed to the final shapes —
knowing, as with new friends,
expressions will begin to cave in
moments after they are made.

Carving's not enough to satisfy.
We search for old trunks
in an attic where dried spiders
bounce in ragged webs rigged
beyond the limits of their legs.
Even bats — ignored all summer —
come on cue, releasing shrieks
cultured on the insides
of our own tight throats.

Opening, we find new bodies
crammed inside the trunks
like joints from bloodless massacres.
Selecting disconnected scraps,
separating tangled arms and legs
shaking out the moth balls
we assemble who we are
but what we want
forgotten.

Masks in place, we mutter and growl,
confronting neighbors face to face
pretending not to recognize them —
judging as they judge.
Discovered, we drift sheepishly
on down the windy street.

Stalking past familiar orange stares
we confuse what separates
the base for grease paint
from an orange shell, and think
how easily they burn out —
how easily they go to pieces.

In the morning
when we gather heads collapsed
in streets or split apart on lawns
we will identify
those who only owned one face
and wore it out on Halloween.

Kathryn Bright Gurkin

NONAGENARIAN

Winters you wake in an arctic bedroom
to drag yourself into a cardigan
and crouched before the one oil stove
begin the endless doing up of buttons.

Noon and the soup seethes in its kettle
like a bad lung. Someone brings food and letters,
laundry, pills. You like to live alone.

What did it mean, the years of planting,
plucking, planting?
No one you know has lived so long.

You have outlived even fear, the treachery
of bone and fat and sinew.
Who would spend his eyes on books
when history is what the heart has known?

Tom Hawkins

MEMO: HOW TO BECOME A FAMOUS WILD MAN

Pick fights; get hurt; bleed on the furniture
(the expensive, not the cheap).
Snore at formal presentations.   Urinate in the punch.
Tell other peoples' teenage children
you're their real father.
Throw a dead cow in the swimming pool,
saw the grand piano in half.
Become peoples' favorite uncouth saint
beside which the dimmest virtue shines.
They will collect your sins
with detailed information
like rare coins.

Tom Hawkins

NINETY-TWO AT NOON

Tractor exhaust wavers
prismatically in throbbing sun
out across earth furrows
rippling like surf.
The chatter of the tractor engine
bounces and burns
across the distance
in chunks audible
and solid as bricks.
The farmer in overalls,
a billed cap and
fully buttoned shirt
swings down from the
tractor seat
and makes some adjustments
at the side of the machine.
Fence posts measure off
the driving past
like reasons why.

Lois Holt

BREAKIN' IN

A mean streak just seems
to run in some families.
It does in mine
down both my arms and legs
can't strap a harness
under my belly
without getting ruptured.
My Ma laced me up once in a corset
like a fine, Southern lady —
pushed my bosom
right up under my throat
until I broke the bridle
ripped and roared
threw that cowboy like a Brahma bull.
He hit the ground running.
Ain't no tinhorn
going to straddle my back
without bustin' butt.

Will Inman
RECOGNITIONS

for Paul Green

early mornings
late afternoons   sun
confident in whole fire
shines through
swelling white figs
yellow in yet green
as if ripe
before their time

sun knows
out of itself
cycles and directions,
sun knows its own sweet fierce
force in green fruit
and is not blinded, as i am,
by great green beetles
in loud orbit
or by the gluttony
of waiting birds

sun
looks into turgid young
(and old!)
constellations of branches,
knows
kin faces opening from earth
skyward in sweet fire,
touches them with harsh
ancient
fresh
hands

and calls them, nameless,
hot core to bursting center,
Thou!

30 July 1981

David Owen Johnson

DUDE BRIDGES

        was a fellow who
had there been a pond called Walden
would have lived on it,
but for lack of a better place
the banks of the fast-moving
mountain streams were his
with names like Santeetla,
Cheoah, Mouse Knob Branch,
The Little Buffalo, and Long Creek.

He was his mother's dear,
everyone knew,
and owned more lore of a woodsman
when he was ten
than the wealthiest
when they die.

His dogs ate up half the county
and he knew of each deer birth
and partridge nest,
could tally up next year's kill,
ration it out so that holidays
would be something special.

Helped increase the family fortune
by spotting the mountain bee,
finding its logged kingdom
and fetching it home in dark,
carrying a queen fertile *ad infinitum*
and her entourage to his father's gums,
creating a state of feudal harmony
unlike Europe ever saw
watched over by a perfect god
to keep their universe, his machine,
in perfect housing, free of disease,
and producing.

It was this sweet money which
produced the Bridges mule,
the Guernsey cow, deed for the house
and Dude wandering under
a low hung moon bringing sparks
from the foxes' bush, making possums
envelop their young, coons to
reach for the sky,
and fish to swim deep
in a pool's dark
which reflected no stars.

His brothers, his sisters,
as prodigious as rabbits,
worked down long rows of summer herbage
and through the spinning blades
and log paths of the gray mill
he always avoided.

His fame: a catfish greater
than them all,
a wild boar from Russia
with tusks four perfect inches long,
no children despite his golden showers,
and a song his mouth sang
deep into equatorial nights
which charmed the heavens
and made honey to flow.

David Owen Johnson

WHAT

    would you do for sex
If you were paraplegic,
Paralyzed, or rolled on wheels?
Fathers, what would be your duty
To blooming libidos of sons
Locked in iron lungs?

Would you say, I have a book
For you
And attach it where
The mirror is above a son's head
Letting him turn pages
Held by rubber bands
With a stick clamped between his
Teeth or come back every
Fifteen minutes
Breathing short from the flood of
Memories going back to your
Fourteenth year when marathon
Masturbation continued sometimes
For months, the brevity of seconds,
Singing in the harmony of hands
Well veined and sprouting finger
Hair — to turn the page for him?

Then would you go to your wife,
Whispering into her ear,
Making the sibilants dance
On the extreme margin,
Sliding down her neck,
The ripple of cold jewels?

Would she know and sit concerned,
Removed, watching some colored
Story, or would she not know
Your breathing had more to
Do with a father's duty,
The regular, steady breathing
Of some metal tank,
Massaging life
Into a form, flaccid
Except in a leaping mind
Hidden inside a head
Which can turn pages
By a magic wand clutched
Between teeth
Incapable of biting
Warm flesh?

Paul Jones

TOWARD SLEEP

Hypnotic, the slow way he moves
Away from light. His arms define
a nest as briars
edge a field. He gathers
straw as if he were a scythe.
The moon pushes him over furrows.
Waves have never been so constant
in their rise and fall. His mouth forms
moans that follow the light. His feet
hold a map from a colder country.

Watch him and remember the boy who
stutters at the newsstand. His eyes
as open as this field, his tongue as tightly
bound as the straw carried for a migrant's
bed. The newsprint on his face where his
mother's kiss might have been like the places
the moon cannot touch when it pushes
a man across a field.

Mary Kratt

ON THE STEEP SIDE

Everything rolled down
in West Virginia.

Our picnic watermelon, toppling from the car,
rolled like a cannonball to the lake,
split, floated like two pink islands.

Potatoes, dug in the garden, tumbled
to the back door. Houses clung
like cicada shells to tree bark.

On the steep road climbing to Mount Hope
coal rose like the torn shoulder of a dark nether giant,
a lanterned miner's hat with a third eye.

Downhill to the mine's wind tunnel
we walked railroad ties on Sunday afternoons,
dug sassafras roots coming home.

We owned the land's crust for house, rhubarb,
potatoes. Underneath belonged to the mine. Blasts
shifted cups in the kitchen.

From Grand View I got the sense that level
was for common people.

In Carolina, where some thought humps were hills
and hills were mountains,
my slant world eye
saved what might have been a level life.

Julian Oliver Long

SALVATIONISTS ESCAPING

The crisis is always the same.
What if, after collecting coats and toys
TV sets, old banana peels, we should slip
broke and walking out of Sherman's Atlanta
barely ahead of gangrenous caissons and burning?

And suppose the children were not
the same every year with surprised grandmothers
getting canned goods and hand me downs, but refugees
with swollen bellies begging the roadside
and sooty fingers plucking our penniless sleeves.

It has somehow to start elsewhere.
The world I make love to has always
had your skin. Its roots and contours
swim in your sea, telling each other touching
all the things that are told.

Yet there is always that other, sometimes
so much of it we die for a while or a lifetime
once as a child I caught the same
tiny fish forty seven times. In Sherman's fires we
swim, tiny fish in buffalo grass.

Love because you must before the world wakes
to the dead city and everything gone but smoke.
Tug at each other's coatsleeves . Do not let go:
as though there were someone to forgive the burning
as though there were someone to love us but ourselves.

Agnes McDonald

CAST/ FOR JASON

Some things
like our lives
are learned early.

You crawl the rug,
hardly out
of your six month's wrapper

to touch the child there,
visitor, his pale flesh,
sad eyes, his cast.

You do not know
the word broken,
or how we heal,
carapace against soft wounds.
Today your fingers
probe the line
where feeling stops.

A child I knew once
asked of every fire truck's
siren screaming
is it coming here?
Lost like wax
that oozes us to mold,
we become our brokeness,

our baby talk bye, bye,
the words that come
later.

Agnes McDonald

EQUINOX

Morning. Light slants
finding its balance.
I dreamed of someone
I loved once.
More nights in dreams than ever
in our lives.

Days shorten now. Earth
and I shift to a more
comfortable spot. From my bed,
I hear a cricket.
Nights will be colder.

Skies like bad opals,
I as heavy as dough.
It is time
to hear sounds that sift
morning.
Time to find
where stars fall,
what hangs on vines to be picked.

Twice you left bowls
of grapes on my table.
Green, red, choices
changing nothing.

Once an old woman across a yard,
air heavy with roses, left
a glass of amber jelly
and two tea crackers on a wall.
Your saying my name was like that.

Michael McFee

HOMING

The sky seems closer, the room more cluttered,
the local foliage more dense and ridiculous
than before, when this was all the world
you knew. Now the instinct is centrifugal,
out and away from the inevitable whining
of television, siblings, idle contradictions.
Yet guilt still remains, the imperative to honor,
the undertow of origin. At home, though not
at home: that ancestral row of portraits
windowing the wall with coffin-black frames
must come down, to be stacked in the attic,
the tiny wire nails in your hammer's claw
leaving holes in the sheet rock as clean
as the pattern on your parents' memory.

Michael McFee

RECLAMATION

In a cornfield near Canton
by an easy bend of the lane-and-a-half blacktop
pebbled with the bed of the nearby Pigeon
leans an old drive-in movie screen.
Kudzu vines thread the braces
loose below and behind, buckling crazy
as the trellis some old lady
tacked on to the ticket booth seasons ago
when her boys took it for a tractor shed.
Panels warped and moonshot, like a drunk
checkerboard, the screen still
looks clear across the corrugated fence
into the next field, where cows cool
in the concession stand. In the shade
men sit on huge wooden spools
the phone company left behind, talking up
the loft, the other three walls
of the tallest barn in Madison County.

Heather Ross Miller

A GIRL WITH MANY MOVING PARTS

Cool, flowing like cool wind over a pine limb,
over sharp hard rocks,
Syrinx — I have no uneven places.
Everything about me and within me is even,
steady-flowing, and cool. *Ocarina*
You made of me mouthpieces and fingerholes,
reeds to suck wind,
sweet tongue and lips to kiss it out again
in a bright crisp bubbling love.

Don't you know how that scared me,
that stumbling chasing wind,
my toes in the sandy river, clinging on, clinging?
You pirate,
you gypsy — passing yourself off a shepherd,
a friend to men and goats and sheep.
I tried to leap the river,
the bright bubbling roar,
but already my toes had taken hold in the shore,
and my knees, my fingers, all my long sweet skin,
turned hollow,
thin, and smooth. *Syrinx!*

Everything tilted a bit,
then swayed,
with a quick important sternness.
I made myself think quick:
> *Starboard Right!*
> *Port Left!*
> *Red to the right*
> *when returning harbor!*

Sunblades cut sharp the dizzying water,
sweeping everything,
sweeping my feet,
sweeping my breath and my lips, mouth, fingers,
and my leap
away from God toward God,
moving,
moving,
moving.

And then, this song and this cool sweet wind,
these lips and fingers fitted so firmly around me,
I loved you again and again and yet again.

Heather Ross Miller

LEDA TALKS BACK TO ZEUS

For the first thing:
    This here is statutory rape.
    I'm a girl under the age.
    You saw me walking here
    in my dreams and clouds and ashes and mudholes.

So, why'd you want to go and do that for?

Sometimes one tree is so tall
only lightning can love it.
That's me, babe, a tall tree courting lightning.
But someday I'll get you back,
you passle of sunbeams, white bull,
you masked man, ridiculous swan!
I'll stand you up against the wall,
you muthafuck! and open a zoo,
packing them in everyday,
and twice on Sunday.

They'll walk around and look at you,
at your thunderbolt and your beard
and your set of York barbells.
And they'll ask: Where's the place to put the nickel in?
                Where's the place to put the nickel in?
                Where's the place to put the nickel in?

You know if I repeat it three times,
it's bound to come true, God-love.

But I still want to know,
why'd you want to go and do that for?
And I ain't never going to stop saying
whoever lost me,
better find me,
right now.

For the second thing:
>You fixed it so I would be right well off,
>marrying money and living in this high rise condominium.
>And I appreciate it, I really do.
>But we lie glued all night in a homey honeycomb,
>and breathe one long black air-conditioned lung.
>The eggshell walls suck inward, out, back in,
>like the ribs of a Japanese fan.
>
>Sometimes I think those kids were made in Japan.
>Look at them: two girls, a set of boy-twins.
>They can speak five languages and rollerskate,
>they drink their bottles and then hold up their arms for love.
>
>Tomorrow I want to throw those kids away,
>and get new kids, like the ones next door,
>plain ones who do nothing.
>
>Rain, now you are making it rain on us again?
>The gutters wallow with living real-wet rain.
>I feel rain pecking inside my brain,
>rain bombing the blacked-out, air-conditioned windowpane.
>
>It rains on the eggshell highrise honeycomb.
>It floods my pastel percale sheet.
>It drowns the kids' clever small bare feet.

Jim Wayne Miller

GIRLS GROW ON TREES IN HAYWOOD COUNTY

Worley ran the rolling store, that big aluminum
box built on the frame of a ton-and-a-half Ford truck,
ran it up half the creeks in Buncombe and Haywood counties.
Folks met us at the big road bringing butter and eggs
they traded for coffee, sugar, salt and plug tobacco.
They traded hides and sassafrass bark for snuff and baking powders,
bloodroot and yellow dock, and a little ginseng,
for needles, can lids, BC powders and toothache medicine.

I rode with Worley the summer I was sixteen, sitting
high in the cab, going the gravel roads that ran
beside the creeks and sometimes through them, roads so little
traveled the center grew up like the balk between untended
cornrows. Worley always tried to fix me up
with girls who came out of the hollers to meet the rolling
store. I half-way liked the ribbing and Worley knew it.

"These hollers is full of gals, good-lookin gals, too!"
His cigarette bobbed up and down, ashes fell
onto the seat between his legs. I was sixteen.
"Yes, sir! Good-lookin gals, by God!" Worley shouted
over the groan of the motor pulling in first gear.

One morning in June on Beaverdam we came
pulling hard around a turn and Worley said, "Looky
yonder!" By a bridge over a branch where a brand new
tin-roofed barn gleamed in a little flat a girl
stood in an apple tree, out on a thick lower limb.
She looked at us and held to another limb overhead.
"I tell you," Worley said, "gals grow on trees up here."

Before we stopped the girl stood on the ground. Worley
swung open the big back doors, climbed up
and took her butter and strawberries, and while she traded,
played matchmaker, told the girl I'd come all
the way up there looking for a healthy gal.
We smiled and felt like fools, the girl and I. Worley
laughed and told it all around how he had
taken me where girls grew on trees, where all
a feller had to do was shake them off like apples.

I remember when they sold the rolling store for junk.
Worley has fallen like ash from his cigarette; the new
barn by the big road is rusty-roofed and weathered,
full of tierpoles dangerously dry-rotted.
The girl who met the rolling store and traded butter
and strawberries may drive a Mustang over a paved road
to the second shift at Enka, Canton, or Hazelwood.

But I still see her standing in that apple tree
in bluejeans and a yellow blouse. I see her barefoot
at the back of the rolling store, with butter and strawberries,
eyes black as chinquapins. I see the maple leaf
design on the prints of butter. — That morning is still as fresh
as the smell of green lumber, bright as the tin roof's dazzle,
as sunlight on new nails in the just-built barn.

Jim Wayne Miller

FEVER

Everywhere the Brier went was music.
Music poured from the porches of holler homes

and fell like flooding creeks out of coves.
Radios and tape decks crooned from thickets.

Cars bouncing over potholed country roads
dodging coaltrucks in noisy showers of gravel

ran filled with red and yellow balloons of song.
Music played from the pockets of schoolchildren,

rose from the jonboats of bass fishermen,
bayed and bawled from coonhunters' jeeps,

from logtrucks growling in the remotest roughs.
Glowing radios, as many as once fireflies

on a summer evening, broadcast a fever.
Even the woods had caught this nervous yearning.

Shirley Moody

THE PAINTER CONSIDERS BLACK AND WHITE

He paints a plowed field
    the parched tint of faded mimosa
    with pale orange furrows.

In this field he paints
    a stooped woman dressed simply in white
    clutching the black wings of a dead crow.
    There are no shadows.

Above them, a pure winter sky.
    This sky gives the painter difficulty:
    flattened with neutral shades,
    a sky too lilac for a Southern haze.

Behind this woman and crow,
    at the field's far edge
    there is the white hint of a church,
    black scratches for windows,
    atop the angled roof two lines
        cross.

There is immediate contrast,
    this black and white,
    which satisfies more than blue and orange
    a placing of flat tones
    next to one another.

Ruth Moose

GOING PRESBYTERIAN

Those white Sundays
I sang with the campfire
Christian soldiers,
Methodist crossed the promised
hands under the beaming voices
of teachers praying us up.
Taught to kneel for wafers
and wine, I felt the stained
glass Jesus with lambs
Mary alone, looking on.

My Baptist grandfather
stretched out his arms
in the river of clinging souls.
They climbed singing
toward the deepest part.
How he praised them all
but my hardshell grandmother
who left footwashings
for others, soft drinks,
telephones, gossip and cigarettes,
kept her lips pure for 99 years.

I chose the descending dove
as far as the chandelier
above the drunken organist
who leans hard on Bach
and rocks the chimes home.
They pass the head of bread
on a silver platter. You pinch
a crumb for your shot glass
four times a year and let
the handful of water
from the altar bowl
take care of the sins
with mercy and grace
and the asking in unison
to please God be included.

Robert Morgan

FIRE WORDS

Because the grounding was faulty for our pump
and well in the old house, we kept away
from the kitchen during storms.
Besides the snap of falling bolts,
then the roll and demolition, there was
a groan in our pipes and banging
as though codes were being sent,
and the crack of some enormous whip
burst from the sink faucet. Mama said
it would kill you just to touch the metal then.
She said a bubble of white fire
blew from the spigot mouth and popped.
I crouched at the dining table hoping not
to see the flash of such electrocution,
dreading the rifle crack within our doors.
Skeletons glowed and buzzed in the lightbulb.
Windows shivered as though freezing in funny light.
Sunday dinner cooled untouched in the dark.
The pipe running from the barn drew down
a hundred yards of voltage from the clouds
and discharged it inside. "That took my breath,"
an aunt gasped each time the sky shorted out.
I could not look upon the fiery face that bloomed
from our plumbing, and squeezed my eyes
and ears to avoid the coming wrath.

Robert Morgan

STRIPES

Where the galluses had hung
over Daddy's sun-bleached shirt
the stripes looked wet with color.
It hurt to think of the midday heat
that scared the khaki white
except for the suspender shadows,
and of the daily salt soakings
and the scrubbings on the board
with bitter soap that chewed
the military fabric soft as flannel.
I've seen the spreading sweat stains stuck
with the cinnamon of nailhead rust
and dry in contour rings across
his back like a record of tides.
The smut markings washed out
in the cauldron redolent with Octagon soap
and troubled by a stick, but the shade
of galluses stayed new like straps
of harness for the long shouldering
of rage in the sun's photography.

Pamolu Oldham

MONGOLOID BOY POEM, APRIL 1981

Each winter I attempt these same lines
about a boy in front of the school for exceptional children.
He wore a blue coat and no hat.
Or was it a blue hat and no coat.
His face was "an empty plate, like a moon lost in a department store."
It was the first snow.
The flakes were large and seldom.
You see his mouth was wide and his tongue out like a slab,
Hungry, I said, for symmetry.

It is April, a Sunday afternoon, unseasonably hot.
My lover is away.
And I am alone with a mongoloid boy pirouetting
among flakes like doilies.
It is a dance of sorts.
My walls are very white, the stove, even the phone.

Sam Ragan

FOR REMEMBERING

I stand at the window and watch
Summer explode across the lawn.
A dog lopes through the meadow,
A bird wings to the woods,
And nothing else moves
On this afternoon
Of summer sun and summer heat.
I turn away and mark it down
For remembering
When these same fields
Are filled with snow.

Salvatore Salerno

SAPPHO

The long chain rattles on the ground.
The Shepherd, not mine,
staked to a yard we share,
paces a worn, tight arc,
breathing a little fog.
She swings like a beacon
from the moonlit door to the trees to me.

I sit, bathed in a guilt not mine.
The owner's away,
caught in that fancy fever
of running from bar to bar
while this wolf's-blood kin
drags her chain beneath the moon,
punished without any sin.

Sirens tear at the evening air
and she howls, echoes of pain.
A blue star throbs above; I want to take her in.
    Go on, howl louder, Sappho —
    cry the blue star down
    to kindle my neighbor's home,
    blazing to call him around.

If this night were a fairy tale
I'd axe that chain
and watch you run to hills
where owners live in a kinder sun.
As it is, I turn my back —
my ears two wounds
in that wordless chant
of the world's grief crying through you.

Sharon Shaw

(UNTITLED)

Insistent and scrappy
and faintly abashed
he ambushed my office every week
sweating his fatigues
and clanking field gear in frustration.
There was this that he had to write.
(He flunked freshman English,
passed C.R.E.P., for the Army
had taught him to circle
one of the above.)
But still
there was this
that he had to write.
It wasn't there at bootcamp,
or hiding on Pork Chop Hill,
not even wasting gooks in Nam.
It was waiting for him stateside
when, age thirty-eight,
he went to jump school.
This was that
that he had to write.
How it felt to fall in space.
He wrote it a thousand ways
on the margins of a hundred Army manuals.
And never got it right.

J. L. Simmons

BACK TO SCUPPERNONGS

For Margaret Boothe Baddour

In the summer, when scuppernongs came ripe,
We shared the secret of your fancy.
Rubber skins parted tartly between
Uncertain teeth to burst sweet pulp
Over our delighted tongues. We spat seeds
Into paper cups and each others' hair.

Scuppernongs yielded to pumpkin spice,
To hot cider freshened with cinnamon and mace.
And we gave you back the pleasure of scuppernongs
Preserved as wine. Not only in a green bottle
Corked against the clock, but jellied
In a hundred poems, preserved in scuppernong tales.

Jane K. Smith

JUKE BOX

The minister's wife
inserts coins of Lifesavers
into wiggly Jeffrey
for five minutes
of Quaker silence.

R. T. Smith

SNAPPER

1.
This afternoon in the shadow of a barn
whose roof reads SEE RUBY FALLS
we bring the painted kettle
of a landed snapping turtle
who went for the red bass lure.
He is older than the farm and
grandfather has never seen one so large.

Since his jaw made its second mistake
and vised the elm limb I held,
he's been at our questionable mercy.
The axe flashes in his flesh.
The black horse cock of a neck,
unfamiliar with the feel of death,
goes crazed in the trampled dust,
hungry for revenge or the memory of thunder.

Then resinous blood drips from the stump,
and cook goes for his knife.
As we perform the predictable chores
daylong boiling gives us soup for supper
more ancient than any contrition
we could whisper for blessing.

2.
Now I roll restless in my bed
surrounded in a nest of feathers
where ancestral shadows wrestle
with dreams of more human sacrifice
as the useless shell in cool grass
by the pump begins to smell.
It is filling with the waning moon.
Nearby cicadas complete the spell.

R. T. Smith

WORKING UP A THIRST IN THE HOLLOW LOG LOUNGE

It's a sign, friend, when the wells
dry up and corn dies on the stalk,
the silks brittle and shucks too dull
to cut your palm. Dust is the word
of the day every day around Lee County
and no church words or fancy science
can alter by an inch the way my lake's
water level drops. Fish won't bite,
maters won't grow sweet. We're eating
beans and okra Mae put up for donation
to some worthy cause at Christmas. Listen,
even the sky ain't right; I been noticing
a streak of green on the horizon every
evening. It's a sign sure as my attic's
the place bats gather. I try to figure
who done wrong and what. I keep my pastures
fenced, my garden weeded. When paint peels,
I strip it and repaint. My tools are sharp
and machines need no more oil. My wife
gets most of what she wants. My tithe
hits the offering basket on schedule.
A man keeps up with the Almanac, despises
vice and keeps his milking barn clean.
He helps a neighbor rick hay, cuts his
meat right on the joint and then the rain
gives up and spoils it all. I'm thinking
I'll have to drill another hole, closer
to the lake and deeper. That's days
of work and no guarantee. The tv says
the sun's a wonder, a miracle, a star,
but I blame it just the same. I mean
here we are, being human hard as we can
and the only thing green on the land
is that thin blade to the west at dusk.

You won't make me accept in quiet
sky's stinginess I can't understand.
What I need's a cool shot glass
of Wild Turkey in my unfisted, dry hand.

Stephen E. Smith

ADVICE

A full moon rose
through the chain-link fence
as my father lifted me over.
The Country Club pool
had been closed since dark,
but there we stood
staring into the pure
star-glazed water of the rich.
"We're as good as they are,"
my father whispered.

He plunged in naked.
I climbed the steel ladder
to the top of the high dive,
crawled to the board's
sandpaper edge and looked down.
What I saw was the bright
moon-struck face of a poor man
who'd had it up to here.
"Jump!" he yelled.

I told the truth: "I'm scared!"
"Listen," he called back,
"you'll never get anywhere
in this life unless you take
a chance once in a while!"
It was the only advice
the old man had ever given me:
I flung myself feet first
into the dark.

Believers, it was like no leap
a poet ever leapt.
I did not hang suspended —
even for a moment —
in the blue drift of air.
I did not see before me
the confused unfolding
of my life,
nor could I hear the voice
of Danny Chapman daring me,
ten years later,
to take the Newcomb turnoff
at ninety.

I did not feel the splintered bones,
the broken promises,
the blackened eyes, the lost love.
And I sure as hell never
saw the fist
that would one night
extract three of my teeth
in the alley behind Sam Loray's Tavern.

No, I dropped straight down
and sank into black water,
belched air at dead bottom,
then clawed my way back
to the night's thin surface.
I looked up into the Milky Way
and saw the bare stars
fewer than my mistakes.

"Help me! Help me!" I screamed.
And from the dark I heard
my father's voice.
"Boy," he said, "you jumped in,
you get yourself out."

Mary C. Snotherly

THE SOUTHERN FRIED CHICKEN

It is not easy telling
even you that I did hide once
behind Aunt Ida's big skirt,
watched her black hand lift
that ax, blade bend the moment's
sun, the fall, the rasp of steel
to bone, and that chicken
thrashing blind about the yard,
spattering Ida's apron red,

and every Sunday's ritual
was the same chicken, fried
deep in fat, rote blessing
of breast for father, thigh
for mother, wishbone for me,

and once in Dellinger's Grocery
I thought I held the tail
of mother's dress, looked up
to see another face —
fear drained me, stiffling smell,
scalded feathers, singe of down.

I am telling you this between
teeth, having dreamed lately
of losing my head, stirring
small red tornadoes with my feet —
saying to you, that chicken
is the only real thing
I have seen die, or dance.

Shelby Stephenson

LOOK AWAY

Cottonleaves redden and the speckled bolls split.
Pickers mark the dew and wait,
lean around the shelters over the machines.
Along the ditchbanks, weeds color slowly, just right
for putting on kneepads, crawling between two rows below the dike.
Hands flourish between bush and sack
toward Lassiter's line, that cool shade.
We lie down under dry stalks,
the hot shimmer of sun leading to dustdark.
Time drops like a shroud.
Gin abandons hoops, hooks, sheets, baggings.
Wagons creak an earthen grace.
Women laugh, hearts melting into cotton.
Gossip floats the room.

Shelby Stephenson

THE ROCK HOLE IN LATE APRIL

The butterflies, reflections alight.
At noon they turn green and yellow, their limbs weaving
when skipper-bugs water the surface.
There is swimming in upsidedown leaves
and one red bobber goes under.
Fallen trees are higher without rain
and the moss looks out of Keats;
yet I know this is Middle Creek,
a place I have carved on these trees
so many times before
I am sentimental.
I cannot raise my voice even when the pole-tip trembles.
In late April I come to watch horsefish roll in the shallow water
under tiny white and black butterflies.
At night the silence wells my eyes
and I make scenes of this place.
The water never is the same spot,
and the paths that lead to my favorite haunts
curve most when the woodpecker sleeps.

Julie Suk

DON'T TELL ME

Don't tell me the dream I've heard
time and again,
the nightmare that fails to catch you
flying, luckily, above it all,
the body jerked up before it lands
sound awake in bed,
the mound a pillow not a grave,
teeth, bones, flesh intact,
the warm breath sleeping next to you,
the one constant.
Don't tell me.
For every dream like that,
another splatters rock-bottom,
and refuses to evaporate.
Don't tell me how we run
slow-motion to escape,
the ground an escalator
winding the opposite way, or worse,
the road we arrive on
going as we come.
Don't tell me the people we meet
flip from face to face.
I believe what I dream.
When the train on the other rail
slides back,
and leaves an illusion of moving forward,
I ride that.
Don't tell me the face at the window
is only reflection,
a life conjured
the moment it flashes by.
Don't tell me it was my mouth pressed against glass.
Don't tell me the mouth is a dream.

Chuck Sullivan

THE ADVENT OF THE KINGDOM IN CAROLINA

By golly damn just
what in the good hell
ever did happen to those
nice folks living in
the about to be repossessed house

Of man who said
the world was a sure bet
to end in the prophetic nick
of time no ifs ands or buts
about it save the selective

Rapture of Christ's glory picking
right hand snatching all true
bumper-sticker believers away dead
in their tracks even from behind
their steering wheels while with His
wrathful left knotted into a rising

Fist He smotes the sorry fallen
rest of us straight way into
the bottomless pit parting our privates
with one holy blow below
the Bible Belt right here
where nothing is

Or could be finer than to spend
doomsday's light saving neither
the day nor the hour in Carolina

Kate Kelly Thomas

MAGGIE YELLS LEROY OUT OF SIGHT

Damn you, damn your fish nets
damn your boat
and damn this shack on stilts
you knowed how I earned my keep
before I come here, you fish-eating sucker!
I cooked your fish
washed your stinking britches
mended your nets
and had your baby
if I'm swamp trash, you're the sucking mud
that pulls me under.

Charles Tisdale

WINTER'S LAST SNOWSTORM

It is too cold for argument, and yet, teeth chattering,
You would have me, walking down this country road,
Explain the reasons for my silence. Winter's last snowstorm
Lashes past the budtips on the trees, stinging my wrists
At the point between pocket and cuff,
The Achilles heel of all casual talkers caught
Empty handed, quite content to let a wincing eyelid
Become the numb imposter of response. Nevertheless,
A few words are in order, and I give them readily,
To resolve the differences, sticking the orange plug on
What for me was a snowman, for you, apparently,
A ghost without a tongue.

Forgive me. I would not presume upon the future
So confidently if this were October and the snow
Falling deeper than my boots. Then we must have talked
A life measured by the words. As it is, barely a tenth
Of an inch scuds like beachsand across the roadway,
Clings on the forsythia and the flowering quince,
Weighs upon their branches the ice sculpture of memory,
Melting — lightest of canvas — beneath the season's warmer pigments,
Its yellow streams of sundrops, firepinks of red.

In this whirlwind of spring, how can you ask me for my word?
I verge near the surface, paying lip service
To the sedative of speech, choosing other than the sound
The certitude of blooms. There is no use for answers
When you and I both see this is winter's last requirement.
Up the road a dog sniffs the shoulders, lean and lonely
For a bone.

Anna Wooten

DIVORCE

I.   Chagall would love this:
your smile tilting the room,
telling me not to lose my way;
the house whirling on its axis.

"Keep stable." And I always have,
it's the rooms that shift,
the furniture that can't come home again.
Outside the yard has crept away
and I turn in time

to see the kitchen, a smutty picaroon,
stuff its pockets and steal through the door.
Thieves. Every room deserts. Even the bedroom,
our bad planet, circles in its rusty orbit
and pioneers away.

I loved you once. Even now I feel it —
something that won't dry up. Bedsprings
in the mind that don't quit. There your
face looms over a martini,
and I see you with many women

spelunking in caverns, skiing away down
snow-covered slopes, a blonde on every side,
a prism in every blonde. Yet I know adventure's
not the way. You'd meet your new love over Scrabble.
She, dark as a library,

would lean and choose a Z.
I am trying my best not to think. I've carried
you in my pockets like incomplete poems
that eat their way to skin; in our young days
have watched your eyes caress my belly

before the kicking males bearing your name
rocketed out of my womb. Now our house
contorts. I feel its columns lurch
and splinter.

II.   Cereal in its box is deathly still. The boys
sleep, two time bombs on the edge of a small poverty.
Tomorrow when they wake the furniture will not know
their names. The walls will not be here to inherit them.
When you are mapping your way to Kansas

I will be having eggs for breakfast, cutting them
quite regularly with a fork. Patting my hair.
The children, twin gravities, will bound in and take
their places, while I hide your name with my knife.
Lying. As if you ever did occur.

Anna Wooten

WHAT AUGUSTINE DID WITH SUNLIGHT

He turned it a particle at a time
(amoebas of light beneath the fingernails),
the whole growing sphere into a vine,
each spine of light a star,
each star a woman,
each woman a huge wonderful bulb
of walking sun.
To turn and watch an action building rings
must be to listen to the water of a deed
washing other deeds, the whole
spectacular plant swaying on a stem
slight as breathing.

CONTRIBUTORS

Betty Adcock lives in Raleigh, North Carolina. Her first book of poems, *Walking Out,* was published by LSU Press in 1975, and won the Great Lakes Colleges Association's New Writing Award. She is completing a second book.

A.R. Ammons is from Whiteville, North Carolina. His most recent book is *A Coast of Trees.* In 1973, he won the National Book Award for Poetry.

James Applewhite is the author of two books of poetry, *Statues of the Grass* and *Following Gravity.* He teaches at Duke University.

Ron Bayes is Writer-in-Residence at St. Andrews College. He is the author of 12 books of poetry and editor of *St. Andrews Review.*

Margaret Boothe Baddour is a former newspaperwoman, English teacher and arts administrator. She teaches creative writing at Wayne Community College and her poems have appeared in *International Poetry Review, Wind, Crucible, Pembroke Magazine* and others.

Mary Belle Campbell is the author of *The Business of Being Alive,* St. Andrews Press, 1982. Her poems have appeared in many little magazines.

Fred Chappell teaches English at the University of North Carolina at Greensboro. *Midquest,* an autobiographical novel in verse, was published by LSU Press in 1981.

Elizabeth Cox lives in Durham North Carolina. Her poems have appeared in *Southern Poetry Review, Greensboro Review, St. Andrews Review, Hyperion,* and others.

Alan Davis teaches at the University of North Carolina at Charlotte. His poems and stories have appeared in *Taurus, Kansas Quarterly, Panache, Southwestern Review,* and others.

Barbara Rosson Davis is one of the founders of *Poetry Center Southeast* at Guilford College. Her poems have appeared in *International Poetry Review, Carolina Quarterly* and others.

Ann Deagon is the author of 5 books. She has a book forth coming from Green River Press. She teaches at Guilford College.

Ann Dunn lives in Asheville, North Carolina. Her poems have appeared in *Carolina Quarterly, Poetry Now, Voices International, Laural Review,* and others.

Millard Dunn was born in Durham and grew up in Wilmington, North Carolina. He teaches linguistics and creative writing at Indiana University Southeast, New Albany, IN. His poems have appeared in *Poetry Northwest, Texas Quarterly, Kansas Quarterly, The Louisville Review, Shenandoah,* and *Stand.*

Charles Edward Eaton is the author of eight volumes of poetry and three collections of short stories. His poetry and prose have appeared in *The Kenyon Review, Bennington Review, Salmagundi, Harper's Magazine, The Atlantic Monthly, The Yale Review* and others.

Grace Gibson teaches at Pembroke State University. She is the author of *Home in Time,* St. Andrews Press. A second volume of poetry has been accepted for publication.

Marie Gilbert is the author of *From Comfort,* Green River Press, 1981. Her poems have appeared in *Internationl Poetry Review, Green River Review, Crucible, Cairn* and others.

Evalyn Gill is the editor of *International Poetry Review.* Her poems and translations have appeared in *Southern Poetry Review, Crucible, Pembroke Magazine, Cold Mountain Review* and others. She is the author of *Poetry by French Women* 1930-1980.

Lucinda Grey teaches in the English Dept. at UNC-Charlotte. Her poems have appeared in *Southern Poetry Review, Tar River Poets, Poem, Green River Review, Davidson Miscellany* and others.

Robert Waters Grey is the editor of *Southern Poetry Review*. His poems have appeared in *Kansas Quarterly, Mississippi Review, Poem, Western Review* and others.

Kathryn Bright Gurkin is the author of two collections of poetry, *Rorschach* and *Terra Amata Poems*. She is at work on a third volume, *The Stainless Steel Soprano*.

Tom Hawkins lives in Raleigh. His poems have appeared in *Kansas Quarterly, Chelsea, International Poetry Review* and others.

Lois Holt lives in Durham. Her poems have appeared in *International Poetry Review, Crucible, Tugboat Review, Writer's Choice* and others.

Will Inman was born in Wilmington, North Carolina. He is the editor of *Kauri,* a bilingual Spanish/English poetry journal. His work has appeared in many little magazines.

David Owen Johnson is head of the English program at Columbus College. He has published in *Black Warrior Review, Carolina Quarterly, Green River Review, Praire Schooner, Texas Quarterly* and others.

Paul Jones has poems in *Ohio Review, Southern Poetry Review, Carolina Quarterly* and *St. Andrews Review*. He lives in Durham.

Mary Kratt lives in Charlotte. Her first book of poems, *Spirit Going Barefoot,* will be published by Briar Patch Press. Her poems have appeared in *Southern Poetry Review, Davidson Miscellany, Tar River Poetry* and others.

Julian Long has had poems in the *Sewanee Review, Pembroke Magazine* and others.

Agnes McDonald has poems in *Southern Poetry Review, Cairn, Tugboat Review* and others. She lives in Raleigh, N.C.

Michael McFee lives in Durham. His poems have appeared in *American Poetry Review, Georgia Review, The Nation, Southern Poetry Review, The Smallfarm* and others.

Heather Ross Miller is the author of seven books, including both fiction and poetry. Her eighth book, a collection of short stories, will be published in the fall of 1982.

Jim Wayne Miller is a native of Leicester, North Carolina. His most recent book is *The Mountains Have Come Closer*. In 1980, he won the Thomas Wolfe Award.

Robert Morgan is from Hendersonville, North Carolina. He is the author of eight books of poetry. His most recent book is *Bronze Age* (Iron Mountain Press 1981).

Shirley Moody lives in Cary, North Carolina. She has published in *The Uwharrie Review, Southern Poetry Review, Cold Mountain Review, St. Andrews Review* and others.

Ruth Moose has published poems in *Amicur Journal, Atlantic, Ohio Review, South Carolina Review* and others. She lives in Albemarle, N.C.

Pamolu Oldham teaches at Fayetteville Technical College. She is the editor of Crains Creek Press.

Sam Ragan is the author of *To the Water's Edge, The Trees in the Far Pasture,* and *Journey into Morning*. He is the Poet Laureate of North Carolina.

Salvatore Salerno has published in *Coraddi, Greensboro Review, Descant, Pembroke Magazine* and others. He is the poet in the Visiting Artists Program.

Sharon Shaw teaches at Sandhills Community College in Carthage North Carolina. Her work has been widely published. Her book, *Auctions,* was published by John Blair.

J.L. Simmons lives in Goldsboro, North Carolina. This is her first published poem.

Jane K. Smith lives in Greensboro, North Carolina. Her poetry has appeared in *More Than Magnolias, Award Winning Poems,* and *Writer's Choice.*

R.T. Smith teaches at Auburn. His most recent book is *Rural Route* (Tamarack, 1981).

Stephen E. Smith teaches at Sandhills Community College. His first book is *The Bushnell Hamp Poems* (Green River, 1980). In 1981, he was awarded the *Poetry Northwest Young Poet's Prize.*

Mary C. Snotherly lives in Raleigh. Her poems have appeared in *International Poetry Review, Crucible, The Pilot, The Lyricist* and others.

Shelby Stephenson teaches at Pembroke State University and edits *Pembroke Magazine.* His book, *Middle Creek Poems,* was published by Blue Coot Press. He will have poems in the *Ohio Review.*

Julie Suk lives in Charlotte and is an associate editor of *Southern Poetry Review. The Medicine Woman* was published by St. Andrews Press in 1980.

Chuck Sullivan is the author of two books, *Vanishing Spices* and *A Catechism of Hearts* (Red Clay Books).

Kate Kelly Thomas lives in Sanford, North Carolina. She has poems in *Poetry Under the Stars* (Moore).

Charles Tisdale teaches at the University of North Carolina at Greensboro. His poems have appeared in *The Antioch Review, The Chicago Review, The South Carolina Review* and others.

Anna Wooten teaches at St. Mary's College, Raleigh. Her work has appeared in *The Lowlands Review, The Southern Poetry Review, The American Poetry Review* and others.